A VOYAGE
TO
ST. KILDA

Being a diary account of a voyage from
Glasgow to St. Kilda
aboard the S.S. Hebrides
during the summer of 1913

Bob Charnley

Maclean Press

First published in the United Kingdom in 1993
Maclean Press
60 Aird Bhearnasdail
by Portree, Isle of Skye
Tel: 047 032 309

All illustrations reproduced
from images within the
'Bob Charnley Collection'

ISBN 0 9516022 5 X

Typeset from author generated disk and printed by
Adlard Print & Typesetting Services
The Old School, The Green, Ruddington, Notts NG11 6HH

DEDICATION

For my good friend Kieran Baxter, a fellow passenger on *Jean de la Lune* during our 1992 summer expedition to St. Kilda.

Would that I could sit on deck - in all weathers - and talk of Peter Pan, and pirates, and crocodiles, and other such wonderful things; and drink my soup, and eat my food, and laugh all the way from East Loch Tarbert to St. Kilda, and not suffer from *Mal de Mer*.

At least the wellington boot didn't drop off *my* foot and fall into the sea at Lochmaddy; but then I am not three and a half years old anymore!

The Editor,
The Bazaar, Exchange & Mart,
Bazaar Buildings,
Drury Lane, London W.C.

February, 1905

Dear Sir,

Could you favour me with a few particulars of St. Kilda Island, off the coast of Scotland?
Are there any means of getting there in the summer? Also what would be the probable
cost? I think of going this summer for a few weeks' holiday. Is there any convenience for
visitors? If so, what does the charge run to? Any other particulars will be acceptable.

Yours etc....

Lancaster, Lancashire.

[The island of St. Kilda lies about fifty miles to the west of Harris. The steamers
"Hebrides" (J. McCallum, 10, Ann Street, Glasgow), and "Dunara Castle" (M. Orme, 20,
Robertson Street, Glasgow), make occasional visits during the summer; but we believe
the journey takes about three days each way from Glasgow. The fare is something like £4
4s., return, including meals. The island is about seven miles in circumference, and is
famous for its wild, rocky scenery, its magnificent air, and the myriads of sea birds that
make their home on the crags, which rise to a height of 1200 ft. sheer from the sea. It has
about seventy inhabitants, a small hardy race who eke out a livelihood by farming,
fishing, and catching sea birds. The village consists of some twenty cottages, a manse, a
kirk and a stores. The cottagers are wonderfully clean and exceedingly kind and
hospitable. We do not know whether accommodation for visitors is available, but the
minister would doubtless tell you whether any of the cottages would take in lodgers; if so,
you can count on simple fare and cleanliness, but you must not expect luxury in any
shape or form, - Editor]

CONTENTS

Front cover illustration:
Children of St. Kilda, 1902. Private photograph.
Rear cover illustration:
The S.S. *Hebrides* in Village Bay, 1902. Private photograph.

Off St. Kilda, August 1992. The Leith-registered Schooner, 'Jean de la Lune'. Comfortable accommodation, superb food and an excellent skipper and crew!

INTRODUCTION

LATE NIGHT PHONE CALLS were a common occurrence during my career as a detective. More often than not the news was bad and required immediate attention with no time to think, just react. But when the phone rang late one evening in June 1992, it was Scottish master-photographer Colin Baxter on the other end, calling from a phone box somewhere in the Shetlands, and I knew I could relax - Colin is *never* bad news!

'Shetland - Land of the Ocean' (Colin Baxter and Jim Crumley, 1992) had just been released in the islands and Colin was preparing to set sail for yet one more destination - Iceland - at 2 a.m. the following morning!

"Would you like to join our July trip to St. Kilda?" he asked, as I heard the small change clink into the distant telephone box. "We sail from Oban on the 25th and will be away for about two weeks."

"Strictly for the birds," was how travel-writer Adrian Bailey had headed his article about the remote island of St. Kilda a month earlier *(Sunday Times – 10 May 1992). "When I went, the sea was rough and half of the dozen passengers were seasick. I had taken the precaution of stuffing myself with Stugeron anti-sickness tablets, staying on deck, and watching dolphins skim under the boat. Unless you know you are a good sailor, you might be wise to do the same."*

My thoughts had wandered back to that newspaper report as Colin, unaware of my personal problem, continued to talk.

"There's no need to give me your decision now; ring the office within the next few days and leave a message for me."

Grateful for some thinking-time I agreed to mull it over, for despite the hundreds of crossings made between Oban or Uig and the Outer Isles I know that sailing is definitely not one of my strong points! I find the five hour voyage from Oban to Barra aboard the massive car ferry *Lord of the Isles* difficult enough if the wind is above breeze-force, so the thought of fourteen days in the North Atlantic on a schooner just 96 feet long did not have instant appeal. However, knowledge of the islands gleaned from books and television is one thing; the opportunity to be able to visit St. Kilda without having to apply for a vacancy with one of the seven annual National Trust for Scotland Work Parties is another, and setting aside all thoughts of personal discomfort I accepted the invitation!

Jean de la Lune - J.D.L. to her many friends - is a 1957 French-built schooner, constructed in oak on oak and displacing some 160 tons. Skippered and crewed by the indefatigable John Reid and Sheila Quillin, I will treasure the memory of those days spent aboard her, enjoying the friendship of some very cheerful companions and eating food of the very highest quality and excessive quantity.

From Oban we sailed via Tobermory, Kyle of Lochalsh and Portree to the island of Harris, interrupting the latter part of the journey with an enthralling two hour stay in the Shiant Isles. At East Loch Tarbert we anchored for the night, sampled some entertaining hospitality ashore, and the following morning made the rough passage to St. Kilda through the bubbling Sound of Harris.

I cannot be too specific about this part of the journey. I am a very good sailor when in a horizontal position, so for me the arrival was far more important than the voyage itself. I only rose from my bunk when I heard the anchor being dropped in Village Bay!

Our party set foot on Hirta at 10.45 p.m. that night. We made our introductions to the Officer Commanding and the resident Trust Warden and then, temporarily ignoring the pleasures of the Puff Inn, I headed for the village street, so visually familiar after years spent looking at old sepia images of the island.

As I stumbled around the deserted homes, the orange glow from the street lights erected by the army did nothing to mar the nostalgia of the moment, for without the presence of the military base how many of us, I venture, would be able to visit this island group? My flag is nailed very firmly to their mast, just below the Union Flag!

On my second 2 a.m. anchor-watch - now a fully experienced seaman - I roamed the slippery deck of *J.D.L.*, watching the meteorites speed through the blackness of the night-sky, whilst ashore the redoubtable puffin-hunters – dark forms betrayed only by the flickering light of their torches - moved between the huts, trying to better the catch of fifty-six birds made the previous night.

*A modern colour postcard of Village Bay, St. Kilda published by Colin Baxter Photography Ltd. and reproduced courtesy of Colin Baxter. From the book **"St. Kilda - A Portrait of Britain's remotest island landscape"** by Colin Baxter and Jim Crumley.*

The rest of my many memories of St. Kilda are personal ones, though I well remember a particularly cold August afternoon when the rain showers came and went in unpredictable waves. One of the *'grasses'*, the delightful, diminutive Fiona - *Fee* to her friends - offered me temporary shelter in the Feather Store, a steaming mug of tea, and the opportunity to play with my favourite piece of modern technology - the most westerly Apple Macintosh™ in the British Isles. And to think, I left Oban secure in the knowledge that I would not need to drive a car for two weeks or touch a computer west of Balivanich. Thanks Fee, I hope the system hasn't crashed!

Along with the writer of the diary and all the other visitors over the centuries, I have now shared the very special experience of a trip to St. Kilda and greatly appreciate the privilege of being able to step ashore in Hirta.

That much maligned author and Hebridean-voyager Alasdair Alpin MacGregor also visited Hirta, his first and only trip to the island being in August 1930, when he arrived *disguised* as the 'Special Correspondent' for *The Times*. His most readable account of the evacuation was published by Cassell under the title **'A Last Voyage to St. Kilda',** but I hope that my maiden voyage will not be *my* last.

8

For the members of the select *St. Kilda Club* - of which I am a proud 'new boy' - the 1913 diary and vintage images which follow will permit comparisons to be made with their own private journals, postcards and photographs, but for the armchair-traveller who has never visited St. Kilda I can only encourage and cajole. If the opportunity should ever come *your* way, grasp it very firmly, don't hesitate, just go. I doubt that you will ever regret it!

Bob Charnley
March 1993

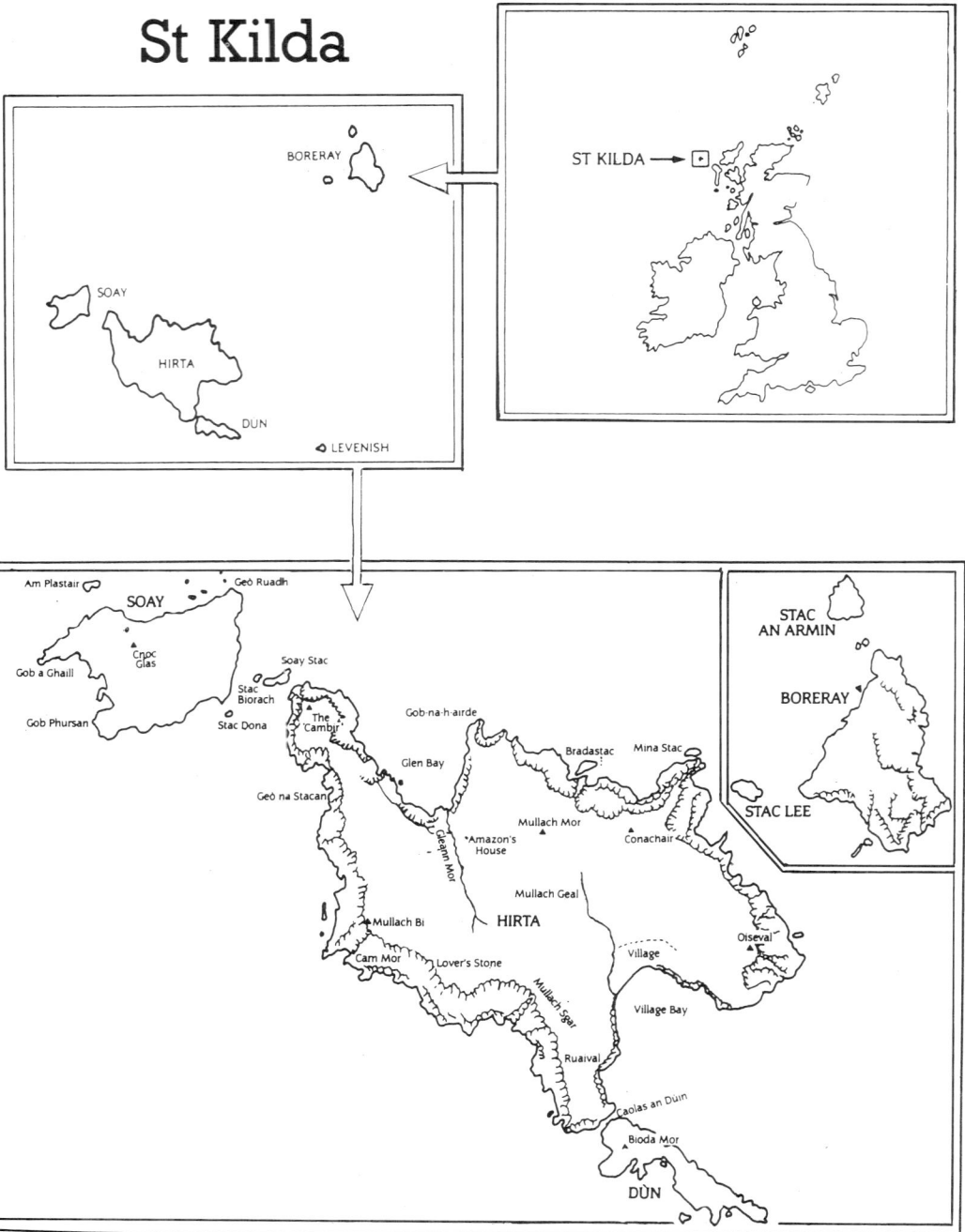

St Kilda

BORERAY

ST KILDA →

SOAY

HIRTA

DÙN

◁ LEVENISH

Am Plastair   SOAY   Geò Ruadh

Gob a Ghaill   Cnoc Glas   Soay Stac

Stac Biorach

Gob Phursan   Stac Dona

The 'Cambir'   Gob-na-h-airde

Glen Bay   Bradastac   Mina Stac

Geò na Stacan

Mullach Mor   Conachair

Amazon's House

Gleann Mor

Mullach Geal

Mullach Bi   HIRTA

Oiseval

Carn Mor   Lover's Stone   Village

Mullach Sgar   Village Bay

Ruaival

Caolas an Dùin

Bioda Mor

DÙN

STAC AN ARMIN

BORERAY

STAC LEE

10

ST. KILDA IN BRIEF

THE CLUSTERED ISLANDS of Boreray, Dun, Hirta and Soay, together with the stacks of Stac an Armin, Stac Lee and Levenish, lie 110 miles west of the Scottish mainland, some 50 miles out beyond the island of Harris. They cover just over 2000 acres and had a population which fluctuated between a recorded high of 180 in the late 17th century to less than 40 in the 1920s. They are better known collectively under the single, magical name - *St. Kilda*.

In May 1930 the islanders petitioned the Secretary of State for Scotland, asking for assistance to leave St. Kilda and for homes and employment to be found for them on the mainland. In August the remaining 36 people were evacuated from Hirta, the deserted islands being left in the possession of their absent owner, Sir Reginald MacLeod of MacLeod.

In 1934, St. Kilda was sold to the 5th Marquess of Bute and subsequently bequeathed to the National Trust for Scotland who accepted the islands in 1957.

Today, St. Kilda is preserved and protected as a National Nature Reserve whilst the buildings and sites of archaeological interest are scheduled Ancient Monuments. Its global importance was recognised by UNESCO in 1987 when they designated the St. Kilda archipelago a 'World Heritage Site'. Other Heritage Sites - the Taj Mahal for example - will be visited by more people in a single day than St. Kilda ever will in two decades or more.

The National Trust lease the islands to the Nature Conservancy Council who, by mutual agreement, sub-lease parts of Hirta to the Ministry of Defence. 1957 saw the arrival of the first Tank Landing Craft with members of Her Majesty's Armed Forces engaged in 'Operation Hardrock', and the slate-grey buildings and radar domes on Hirta are testament to the continuing presence of the officers and men of the St. Kilda Detachment, Royal Artillery Range (Hebrides), Benbecula.

Because of its geographical location, St. Kilda receives few *casual* visitors but everyone is expected to report to the Officer Commanding and the resident Trust Warden on arrival. It is more than just a common courtesy, it is essential for the good management and preservation of the island; byelaws exist and the visitor should be aware of the penalties for infringement.

The Trust may refuse entry to any person without reason and byelaw offenders *"shall leave the Reserve forthwith by the next available civilian transport or Ministry of Defence transport if available, if instructed to do so by the Warden..."*; a Summons may result as a consequence of any malicious or wilful act, with a fine, on conviction, not exceeding £20.

Truly, St. Kilda is a world apart.

It boasts the largest colony of gannet in the world; the largest British colony of fulmar; more than half the British population of puffin, plus guillemot, kittiwake, Leach's petrel, razorbill, shag - the list is endless. More than 200 books or reports have been written about St. Kilda - a positive indication of its impact on the voyager - but a useful introduction to the island, its landscape, weather, natural history, archaeology and history, is the National Trust for Scotland's own 95 page offering **'A St. Kilda Handbook'**. This, then, is St. Kilda in brief.

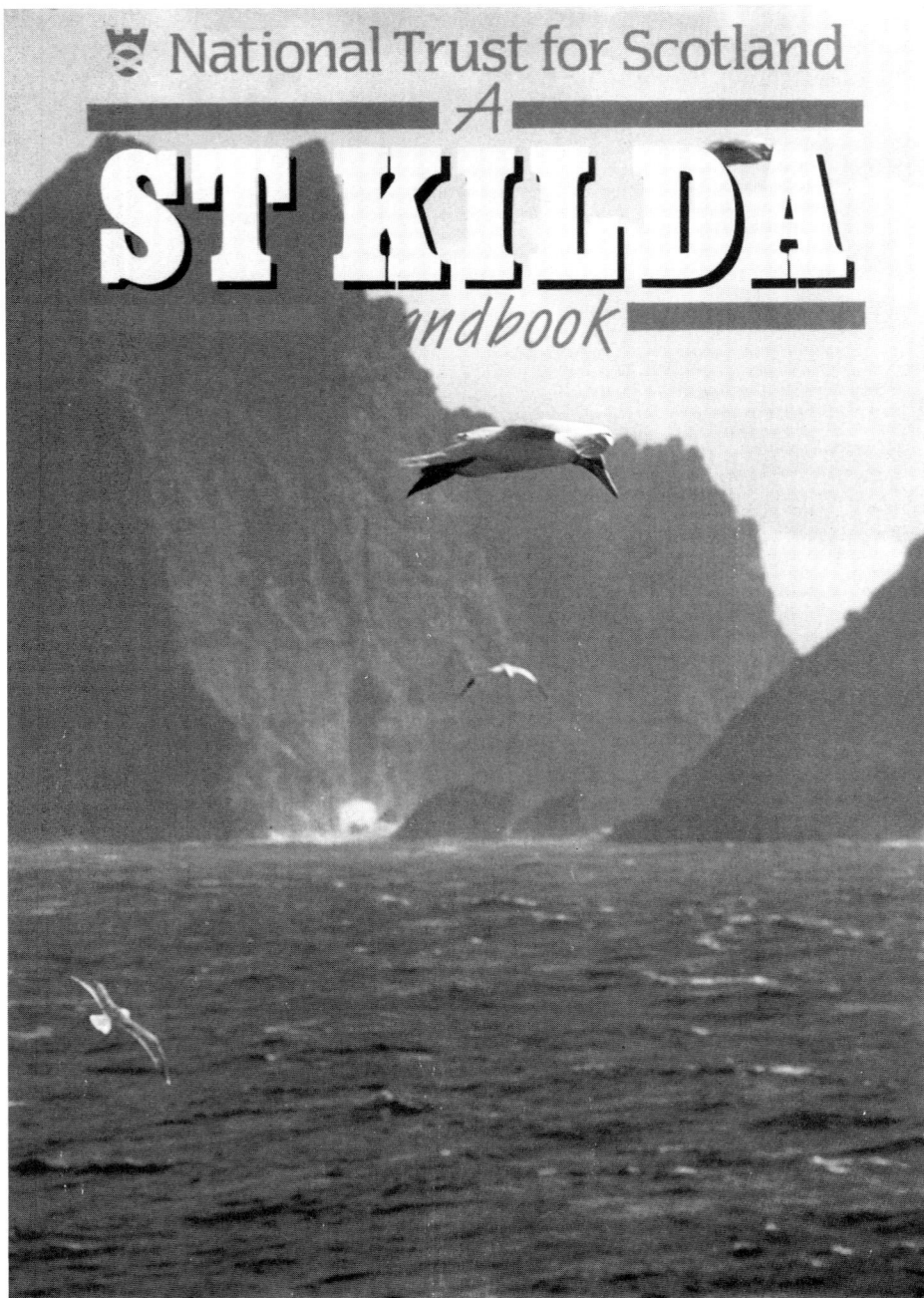

National Trust for Scotland
A
ST KILDA
Handbook

ABOUT THE DIARY AND PICTURES OF ST. KILDA

IT WAS AS A COLLECTOR of early photographic images of the Highlands and Islands of Scotland, that I was asked by Glasgow-based publisher Richard Stenlake to put captions to some of my vintage postcards of the islands of the St. Kilda group. The result was a small but well-received picture-book **'Last Greetings from St. Kilda'** *(Stenlake & McCourt 1989, reprinted (twice) 1992),* illustrated with over 40 views of the islands taken by. various photographers over a fifty-year period from the 1880s to the final days before the evacuation in August 1930.

But, as the pages of that book were passing through the printing press, a typed journal - 27 A4 size sheets held together by a large metal tag - came into my possession. It arrived from a Scottish dealer who had received it via a dealer in the south of England, the latter having considered it to be interesting but of little consequence. Although the journal/diary is unsigned and undated, the first line entry *'Beccles, Friday, 22nd August',* coupled with a later reference to the *Daily Mirror* wireless man and the *'Daily Mail flying man...',* dates the item to that last summer of peace - and of life for so many - 1913.

The anonymous writer describes his journey from Beccles in Suffolk to St. Kilda, via Edinburgh, Glasgow, Islay, Oban, Mull, Coll, Tiree, Skye and the Outer Isles. Sometimes he is concise and informative, at other times lengthy and repetitive, but as a contemporary account by an observant tourist, it gives a delightful insight into a typical voyage aboard the S.S. *Hebrides* in the early years of this century. It also contains a few interesting details about life on the island which can now be added to the great St. Kilda melting-pot of fact and fiction, truth and error.

Because so much has been written about this island, myth becomes fact and errors tend to reappear in later volumes. Many hours go into any research but we all err, and the reader should not be too quick to criticise.

When the picture of three islanders on an exhibition stand *(illus.1)* appeared in **'Last Greetings...',** the caption referred to the photograph as having been taken in *1935* and quite a number of people took me to task, pointing out that the same picture had been used in an earlier book on St. Kilda where the author had stated that the demonstration of spinning and weaving took place on the St. Kilda stand at the Bellahouston Exhibition in *1938.*

The picture is on a postcard which was posted at Lochmaddy, North Uist, and the postmark clearly reads *22 August 1935.* The sender writes *"We managed to land at St. Kilda. The deserted houses present a sad spectacle...".* A souvenir cachet, applied to this postcard - either on the island or on board the steamer whilst on the return passage - is dated *20 August 1935,* which suggests that the actual photograph was probably taken at the Jubilee Exhibition held in Glasgow's Kelvin Hall in 1935.

In **'A Voyage to St. Kilda'** you will read the 1913 account of our English traveller to the island and view a selection of pre-1930 images which compliment the text. The diary itself has been edited and corrected, but this will not reduce your pleasure as you travel down the Clyde with the voyager, enjoying the stops en-route to St. Kilda before the return trip to Glasgow via South Uist and that most beautiful of all Hebridean islands, Barra.

In particular you will see picture postcards of St. Kilda produced over a thirty year period and aimed solely at one market - the inquisitive tourist. Produced in their thousands, they were sold on board *Dunara Castle* and *Hebrides,* at ports along the route and on the island itself. Some of the cards are rare and are much sought after by fellow-collectors, only occasionally coming onto the open market through specialist dealers and philatelic auctioneers. Also scattered amongst the text - and at the end of

1. Evacuated from Hirta in 1930, these former islanders, Neil Gillies, Donald Ferguson and Mary Gillies, demonstrate their skills on an exhibition stand in the Kelvin Hall, Glasgow in 1935. A sepia postcard posted from Lochmaddy in August 1935, the writer ends her message, "We had a really rough sea going out to St. K. but it was fun."

the book - are some previously unpublished private photographs, taken in 1901 by an unknown passenger bound for St. Kilda aboard *Dunara Castle*.

With some of the postcards it is not always possible to accurately pinpoint the year in which the photograph was taken. Many publishers used late Victorian images, exposed on glass plates in the 1870s and 1880s - before the dawning of the first British *pictorial* postcard in 1894 - to produce Edwardian postcards, and the public accepted this money-saving deception, often failing to check the reality of the landscape, or the dress of the inhabitants, with the actual card in their hands. Occasionally a determined postcard-salesman persuaded a Hebridean post-master to buy more cards than he could possibly sell in a decade, never mind within the season, and one card re-enforces that point. *(illus.2)*.

Titled *'Bala, Eriskay, where Prince Charlie first slept in Britain'*, this Gaelic-series *Cairt Phostail* was produced around 1902-03 from a photograph taken by Archie Chisholm - the Procurator-Fiscal in Lochmaddy at the time - and more details about Chisholm, plus further examples of his work, appear in **'The Western Isles: A Postcard Tour - Barra to North Uist'** *(Maclean Press, 1992)*. In June 1907 a Mr Harry Wright posted this card from Oban to his mother in Dunbar. Assuring her that he and Ethel were safe, Harry continued:

'The Captain is very fond of the bagpipes, but very few passengers on board to St. Kilda…' The two facts were probably not related in any way!

In my collection, alongside Harry's postcard, there is a second copy of the same card, identical in all respects save for the date it was written. Cancelling three stamps with a total value of two and a half old pennies (1p), the card was posted from Nairn to an address in Sidcup, Kent, on 23 August, *1959!*

Now that *is* a long shelf-life for a postcard, and fifty years from now it might create some problems for the photographic researchers!

14

Bala, Eriskay, where Prince Charlie first slept in Britain. (Copyright)

2. *A Cairt Phostail of Bala, Eriskay. Produced circa 1902 for the Edwardian tourist market, copies of this particular card were still being sent through the post over half a century later.*

"As soon as the windless had ceased to rattle and the last bag of meal was aboard, we dropped down the Clyde and steamed away to the North."
[Richard Kearton: "With Nature and a Camera" 1897]

THE DIARY

1. From Beccles to Glasgow
and a trip down the Clyde

Beccles, Friday 22nd August

WE LEFT BECCLES at 9.55 a.m. for Glasgow via Norwich, Doncaster, York, Newcastle and Edinburgh; changed at Haddiscoe and at Norwich. Saw Ely Cathedral at a distance. It was a lovely trip through the Fen country where we saw water and corn mills with 4, 5, 6 & 7 sails!

The harvest was in full swing in the Fens and we passed some splendid crops of wheat and barley. At Lincoln we stayed some time; the Cathedral looked fine. New to see the kids hanging about on the meadow - just opposite where the train stopped for ticket collecting - turning somersaults for coppers! We could get hardly any decent grub; worst refreshment arrangements ever, and dirty, and the lemonade was the worst in the world.

Saw the cathedral at York and changed trains but found that we could get no connection for Glasgow so we had to wait one and a half hours for a train to Edinburgh, where we arrived at 11.15 p.m. but could get no further. We stayed the night at the Caledonian Hotel which was exceedingly comfortable. Colonel Macgregor, with Iain and Jessie, met the train and came and had a chat at the hotel, and saw us again the next morning; then we took the train to Glasgow where we arrived at 1 o'clock.

Stayed at the Ivanhoe Hotel in Buchanan Street; we made a mistake in the hotel but it did not matter much. After lunch we went on the trams around Glasgow, then to two cinema shows and the Palace Music Hall. Never saw so many people and trams in the street.

This being Saturday night a large number of the youths of Glasgow were suffering from the *Scottish wine,* or rather too much of it. Saw several 'lunatics' returning from a football match. They have the fever badly here and betting is rife - also badly. The sooner this is stopped the better. I hear that the Territorials suffer much in numbers from the keenness displayed by footballers"

Sunday 24th August

"What looked like the promise of a wasted day in Scotland turned out to be one of the most delightful surprises of the trip.

On having my usual chat before going to bed, I found that although the Scots have a reputation of 'keeping' the Sabbath strictly, there was advertised a trip down the Clyde by the *Isle of Cumbrae* from Jamaica Bridge (Buchanan Line) to Rothesay, Dunoon, Kyles of Bute and Loch Striven. We took advantage of its only costing 3/6d each.

We started at 10.30 a.m. and saw some well-known big liners and several large ship-building yards - Fairfield Shipbuilding Co., Mackie & Thompson's Ship Yard, Hendersons, Barclay, Curle, Connell & Co., Armaments Co., Yarrow & Co. Ltd., and John Brown & Co.

In these yards there seems to be a tremendous amount of building going on of ships of large size. We saw the enormous *Aquitania*[1] being finished off. There also seems to be a number of gunboats and torpedo boats being finished at Yarrows and

[1]*Aquitania* acted as a troop-ship during World War I, sailing to Gallipoli in the summer of 1915.

elsewhere. We passed the celebrated Partick Saw Mills, Clyde Valley Electric Power Station, foundry of John Reid & Co., Merblands Foreign Cattle Wharf, also the entrance to the Great Queen's Dock with its N. & S. Basin full of large ships. The opposite side of the river is Princess Dock.

The new Sewage Works of Glasgow at Shield Hall are of very large area and when finished will cost millions; they say it will take 25 to 30 years to clear the river, and I should say it would. The river at Jamaica Bridge, and the River Bridge from which we started, appeared to be composed of *ink,* although the gulls seem to thrive on what it contains. They rocst on the top of the goods sheds by the side of the landing stations.

The people on our boat seem to be Glasgow people of a type bent on a Sunday outing, most going to Dunoon and Gourock, a few to Rothesay, and a very few on the complete trip to the Kules of Bute. We saw Govan - having taken in a few more passengers - and then the Sewage Outfall Works at Dalmuir to Bowling. Here we saw the entrance to the Forth and Clyde Canal.

Length 901 ft.   Breadth 97 ft.   R.M.S. AQUITANIA   Tonnage 47,000.

3. "We saw the enormous 'Aquitania' being finished off."

We then made for Dunoon situated on the lovely shore of Argyll. Here we unshipped several passengers, to pick them up on our return. Saw a man badly hurt, I'm afraid, by being squashed by the landing stage on leaving. The houses all along to Inellan are situated on the edge of the hill near the sea and look perfectly situated for a summer's holiday position. We passed Castle Toward and Toward Lighthouse and we had a view in the distance of the Isle of Cumbrae at the entrance of the Clyde.

But we made for Rothesay and here everyone seemed to be out to await the arrival of the boat. We lost most of our passengers together with those we had left at Dunoon.

I heard afterwards that Dunoon and Rothesay are not like Glasgow where the public-houses are closed all Sunday, but we saw no signs of the fact when they came on board in the evening. The boat we were on was also 'Tee-To' for the day, worse luck!

18

The sea-gulls were prolific and everyone seemed to encourage and feed them; they seemed to appreciate it, - quite four types of gull were seen. Rothesay is also seemingly a perfect summer spot and is in Bute - the Marquis of Bute living in his castle a little further inland. The sea here was dark blue and at times showed signs of emerald green. Yachts seemed to be everywhere, large and small.

We then left Rothesay and steamed down the Kyles of Bute - a more lovely trip I have never been on in Scotland.

4. Rothesay. "...and here everyone seemed to be out to await the arrival of the boat."

The shore rises on both sides gradually to a considerable height, the rocks suddenly stopping to a height of some feet at the shore. We passed Port Bannatyne and then on to Ormidale, a treasure of a place for loveliness so near a town like Glasgow. We then passed through a narrow passage into Loch Striven and to Rothesay Pier again and later on we picked up our passengers we had dropped there for a drink earlier in the day. Returned in the evening by the same route to Jamaica Bridge and landed, having spent a most enjoyable Sunday, and having seen what to me was one of the most pleasant surprises of the trip."

"The chief drawback to sailing in these small steamers, in my opinion, is the poor character of the sleeping accommodation ... they should put over the Cabin door - "All ye who enter here leave Pride behind." You had to crawl into your berth head foremost, and then *whummle* out as best you could". [The Revd. Roderick Lawson: from his one penny, 24 page pamphlet "Flight to St. Kilda" written after his voyage to the island aboard the SS *Hebrides* in July, 1902]

2. On the 'Hebrides' to Tiree via Oban and Mull

Monday 25th August

WENT INTO GLASGOW after breakfast and bought a few stores - tobacco, sea-sick preventatives, green apples, &c. Came to the conclusion that the streets and shops were the best we had seen - better than the London shops. We finished in the morning with a cinema show, of course.

Having returned to the hotel and paid the bill we took a taxi and went to number 44 berth at the Quay.

LANDING STAGE AT BROOMIELAW

5. A chromo-lithographic postcard issued for the Glasgow International Exhibition of 1901 showing the Landing Stage at the Broomielaw, Glasgow, departure point for so many sea-voyages.

Went on board the *Hebrides* s.s. at about 1.45 p.m. The boat should have started at 2 o'clock but it did not get away until 4.15 p.m. so I watched the cargo put on and saw our fellow trippers come on board. Saw our cabins - the Mrs. in Ladies, number 1 berth, with myself in number 26 berth in opposite Men's section. There are six bunks in mine - mine being on the top near the porthole.
One man suffering from Glasgow Scotch wine - apparently an Agent for a Distillery (McLachlan's) - turned out to be a large Glasgow baker and confectioner, and brother-in-law of the great ---M.P.---[2]

We started at last down the Clyde; a most interesting trip with plenty of noise from riveters at the shipyards. Saw the *Sardinian* arriving from Canada.

Stopped at Gourock and took in more passengers and I went ashore for a time - we took in a lot of cargo from the *Daily Mirror* for St. Kilda, also the *Daily Mirror* man for the wireless telegraphy.

[2] Whilst the writer identified this M.P. the publishers would prefer that he remains anonymous to save possible embarrassment for the relatives of his brother-in-law.

6. S.S. Hebrides. *Built in 1898 for John McCallum & Co. of Glasgow, she sailed extensively around the West Highlands and Islands delivering a variety of cargo to remote Hebridean ports, many now deserted and only visited by the occasional yachtsman and woman. During the summer months she carried fare-paying passengers, and the Western Isles became just a little more accessible to the tourist. On the late summer trips passengers usually had to compete for return journey space with the island sheep, being shipped in their hundreds for the mainland market sales. This fine vessel was scrapped in 1955.*

Visit the ROMANTIC WESTERN·ISLES and LONE St KILDA

7. *The cover of John McCallum's 16 page brochure for their summer tours aboard the S.S. Hebrides. It contained the following information for the benefit of the passengers. "Ladies are accommodated in Ladies' Cabin and Ladies' Four-berth State Room, which communicates with Ladies' Cabin. Stewardess is always in attendance, and special attention is given to ladies travelling alone ... Servants travelling in Cabin of Steamer pay full Cabin fare ... It is desired that Passengers retain the same seat at meals during the voyage. The Chief Steward is to see that, during the day, the ports are open when weather permits. No passenger is allowed to change his State Room or Berth, nor to open the port holes, without the knowledge and permission of the Chief Steward."*

ANNUAL CRUISES TO ST. KILDA

St. Kilda Bay.

Main Street, St. Kilda.

St. Kilda Village.

ON SPECIAL DATES.

FARE FOR THE TRIP,
BOARD INCLUDED :

£10

Berths in Four-Berthed Room, 2/6 extra; in
Two-Berthed Rooms and Deck Cabins, 5/-
extra; and Passengers remitting by own
Cheque (London excepted), will please
include cost of exchange.

The Tour occupies about 7 days, but any
meals supplied beyond 8 days to tourists
will be charged at the rate of 9/- per day.

EARLY BOOKING ADVISABLE.

STEWARD'S RATES :

Breakfast, ...	3/-
Dinner, ...	4/-
Tea, ...	3/-

FIRST-CLASS CUISINE.

St. Kilda—Cliffs, 1,250 Feet High.

8. A page from a pre 1920 brochure, produced by McCallum & Co. to advertise their tours to St. Kilda.

On the quay we were much amused by a man named 'Larky' who seemed to be rather an old man who was made a butt of, and seemed to make him useful. We then steamed by Greenock, Dunoon, Rothesay, and at dusk passed Isle of Cumbrae, Largs, Saltcoats, &c., past the beautiful Isle of Arran, and at night round the Mull of Kintyre.

Within sight of the lighthouse on Rathlin Isle (Ireland) some people, including myself, were rather bad; I could not go to bed as the berth was too small so I tried to sleep in the saloon by the sideboard, but it was a failure. We passed between Jura and Islay and stopped at Port Askaig where we dropped some cargo. It was early morning and everything looked quite beautiful - the water clear down to about 20 feet. The fish looked very plentiful - lythe and cuddies seemed to prevail.

9. 'Port Askaig, Islay, from the Sound.' *"We passed between Jura and Islay and stopped at Port Askaig where we dropped some cargo."*

We then passed on to the open sea, and to the isle of Colonsay and stopped off by the Port Scalasaig Inn there, and a boat came from the small bay on which was a quay, and brought several persons who had been staying at the Hotel playing golf. The boat was now full.

10. 'Scalasaig Hotel, Colonsay.' *... stopped off by the Port Scalasaig Inn there, and a boat came from the small bay on which was a quay, and brought several persons who had been staying at the Hotel playing golf."*

We took our cargo of fish to Oban, and the passengers also who were bound for that place. We passed the Isle of Scarba (a big mound) and some weird isles called Isles of the Sea, looking very ragged, having a fine coast view of the Rose of Mull on our left, part of the Isle of Mull; then went between the Isle of Kerrera and the mainland. This Sound of Kerrera is very pretty. We reached the Bay of Oban - it was looking lovely on a summer's morning, with several large yachts, including the *North Star* &c.

Oban is situated all around the bay facing west, and in the centre, on the top, there are some ruined unfinished buildings which resemble a coliseum; on the left of the bay, looking at it, are the ruins of Dunollie Castle.

11. 'Oban Bay.' "*Oban is situated all around the bay facing west, and in the centre, on the top, there are some ruined unfinished buildings which resemble a coliseum...*"

After going round the town and buying a few things we started off again. The steamer, having landed her cargo and taken on more passengers, passed out of the bay in the direction of the Sound of Mull, leaving Dunollie Castle on our right. I hear that Oban is not quite so fashionable as it was because such steamers as ours have opened out so many of the Isles of the Hebrides - such as North and South Uist - lately. People prefer going further afield now, especially as they can get to and from the places in reasonable time.

We passed Loch Etive then the Isle of Lismore, a long low isle covered in one part with sheep &c.; the end nearest to Mull is surmounted with a lighthouse showing the entrance to the grand Loch Linnhe which goes to Fort William and is a very fine specimen of a Highland sea loch. We saw Castle Duart on a point opposite Lismore light and the scenery was typical all the way to Tobermory, where we brought up and dropped cargo.

The *Daily Mirror* man says he is going to shoot sea-gulls! I tell him that this is no sport and persuade him to confine himself to just two specimens of each gull. Tobermory is in a bay in a most delightful situation as we go gradually to the quay, or pier. The well-known boat *Chieftain* leaves and we bring up in her place. The Tobermory Whisky Distillery is situated on the left looking at the town, and the houses are in a circle around the bay, and a little behind the town on the hill is the Government Wireless Telegraphy Station.

12. 'Tobermory looking South.' 'Tobermory is in a bay in a most delightful situation...'

We went ashore to look around and chatted with two policemen &c. We saw a woman (Mrs. Cameron) who kept a grocers shop and who came from Applecross and Biddy was on her track at once to chat with her. Standing with our backs to the town and looking across the bay we have a very pretty waterfall on our right, and across the bay is Castle Aros belonging to a Mr. Allan of the celebrated shipping line.

The Spanish Armada ship, the *San Floriza,* was sunk here - about 100 yards in front of the pier, in what is now 60 feet of water and about 20 feet of mud.[3] Dredging operations have taken place for some years and have now been given up. They found some old metal guns, swords and pewter plates and a few silver coins but no gold. It cost them more than the stuff fetched in London, in spite of the high prices - the few finds of plates made over £10 a piece. Beyond the fact that they found conclusive evidence that the ship was sunk here, they found very little to justify the expense of trying to dig relics from it. How she was brought into the Bay is a bit of a mystery.

We left Tobermory at about 4 o'clock and arrived at Coll by 7.30 p.m. It is a very desolate-looking isle with no trees; a very dull place. A picturesque ferry boat, black in colour, came out to meet us. There is a good church here and a few houses clustered near the pier head which we did not go to. After landing some goods and taking in milk we went further down the 'Little Minch' to Tiree, also seemingly desolate and tree-less. A person who was landing there said that they were cutting the island up into small holdings. I hope the small-holders will not be allowed to starve - but I suppose the generous Government will come in and assist the holders with more money, if they want it, from out of us poor professional milch cows.

[3]This Spanish vessel sank in the bay in 1588, allegedly blown-up by John Smollett, an agent of Francis Walsingham's English Secret Service

13. Black-houses at **Boust,** Coll, in the early years of the century" ... a very desolate-looking isle with no trees; a very dull place."

14. 'Scarinish Harbour, Tiree.' "...we went further down the 'Little Minch' to Tiree, also seemingly desolate and tree-less. A person who was landing there said that they were cutting the island up into small holdings. I hope the small holders will not be allowed to starve...". An early 1900s postcard produced from a photograph taken by the author Erskine Beveridge.

We arrived off the landing places - which are near the lighthouses - after dark and a big ferry boat (holding about 10 tons they said) came to meet us, and accompanying it was a small rowing boat with two or three passengers, including Mr. MacArthur the St. Kilda missionary; a smaller ferry boat also came out.

After taking about three-quarters to one hour putting the cargo on board the ferry boat and taking in some bales of salted cod and haddock for North Uist, we left for Carbost in Skye.

15. *Tiree, and safety at sea was not of prime importance in 1901. Thirty-two people - plus luggage - fill the boat! A private photograph, taken from the deck of 'Dunara Castle' outward bound for St. Kilda.*

The journey across the Little Minch was fairly good. We passed the Isles of Rum, Eigg and Muck on our right, also one called Canna. The *Daily Mirror* wireless-man is a Portuguese named F. Figuardo, and he is booked to be at St. Kilda for about 3 to 4 months. The range of his instrument is about 80 miles and his receiving station is at Lochboisdale, South Uist, which is being finished on Saturday next by the *Daily Mirror* people. He says he only took this job on Thursday last and tells me that he was only provided himself with 12 bottles of Lemonade essence and a few medical comforts &c. Some people are easily satisfied!

I forgot to mention that before we reached Oban today we passed Lord Strathcona's yacht; they said (which I doubt) that he was standing on the deck at the time. The Oban people were all expecting the *Daily Mail* flying man Hawker to come at 4 o'clock, it being one of the stops in the great £5,000 Round the British Isles flying competition. To win the prize he has to be in Dublin by 7 o'clock - good luck to him. I saw by the papers that he had reached Northumberland by yesterday evening.

This is the longest day I think I've ever spent, and certainly one of the most enjoyable, in country which I wanted for years to go and see and places I wanted to visit. May the rest of the days of this trip be as interesting!"

"We had an hour at Dunvegan Castle ... although somewhat old-fashioned externally, the rooms are comfortable and contain some relics of the Jacobite rising ... the lady who showed us through the house was a German, who spoke English so badly that it was next to impossible to know what she said." [The Revd. Roderick Lawson: from his one penny, 24 page pamphlet "Flight to St. Kilda" written after his voyage to the island aboard the S.S. *Hebrides* in July, 1902]

3. The Isles of Skye and North Uist

Wednesday 27th August

WE ROSE EARLY having spent a quiet night and gone to bed very sleepy. We slept soundly and had a good night's rest, waking up just as we were entering Soay; here we stayed a short time discharging more cargo and then made our way to Carbost.

We passed in sight of the coast, which was grand, reaching the entrance to Loch Bracadale about 45 minutes later, passing the two bluff heads which guard the entrance, one of which has three rocks standing up which are called MacLeod's Maidens.

The celebrated Talisker Distillery is at the top of the Loch and we went to have a look at it, but it did not give us a great impression - the place seemed to be under repair. After taking several casks of whisky aboard, which of course we could not touch, and taking photos of two pretty Highland girls we started back down the loch on the way to Dunvegan and Colbost.

16. 'Carbost from the West.' "The celebrated Talisker Distillery is at the top of the Loch and we went to have a look at it, but it did not give us a great impression - the place seemed to be under repair."

We entered the Loch of Dunvegan about 12 o'clock and sailed close to the rugged and lofty coast past Dunvegan Head and ultimately reached Colbost - which is situated in a small bay off the main loch. There is no pier here and the usual 'big' ferry boat brought some goods and we gave them more. We then passed out of Colbost bay and went on to Dunvegan which is situated a short distance further on. The water here was beautifully clear.

We moved up the loch and had a grand view of Dunvegan Castle on our left front. We went out and brought up at the pier where we landed and saw what there was to be seen. A few women were gutting herring similar to what we see them do at Lowestoft and Yarmouth. They were rather ancient and were most shy, especially when their photos were asked to be taken.

Dunvegan Castle

17. 'Dunvegan Castle.' *"We moved up the lock and had a grand view of Dunvegan Castle on our left front."*

This port seems to be the port of embarkation for the Outer Hebrides; to North and South Uist from Skye via Portree or to Loch Alsh via Kyleakin. We left Dunvegan at about 2 o'clock and crossed the Minch to Locheport in North Uist. Here we were pleasantly surprised; the entrance was a very narrow one with two mountains on the right entrance and one on the left not far off.

The rocky coast was very grand and I should say that the Captain of the *Hebrides* must have been a careful navigator to take a boat, even of the size of ours, through such a channel. After going some distance the land is very much lower and the loch is fairly populated on the south side for these isles. The farms, or small holdings, do not show any signs of harvest. We were soon surrounded by boats again. The ferry or inland cargo boat was a much larger one than usual and took in a large quantity of stores apparently taking a long time to take them on board.

This boat goes all over the inland part and distributes what it has on board to the inhabitants. We also met a number of boats containing women selling home-made Harris Tweed. It looked very good and several passengers bought some for 3/3d per yard. It takes 7 yards for a suit and 8 yards for a dress. These boats, about 8 or 9 in number with the ferry boats, looked very pretty in the evening light sailing away from the ship.

Steamer "Hebrides" at Locheport North Uist. D.R.M.

18. 'The Steamer "Hebrides" at Loch Eport, North Uist.' *"The rocky coast was grand and I should say that the Captain of the 'Hebrides' must have been a careful navigator to take a boat, even of the size of ours, through such a channel."*

Loch Eport Ferryboat

19. 'Loch Eport Ferryboat' *"...crossed the Minch to Locheport in North Uist. Here we were pleasantly surprised; the entrance was a very narrow one with two mountains on the right entrance and one on the left not far off."*

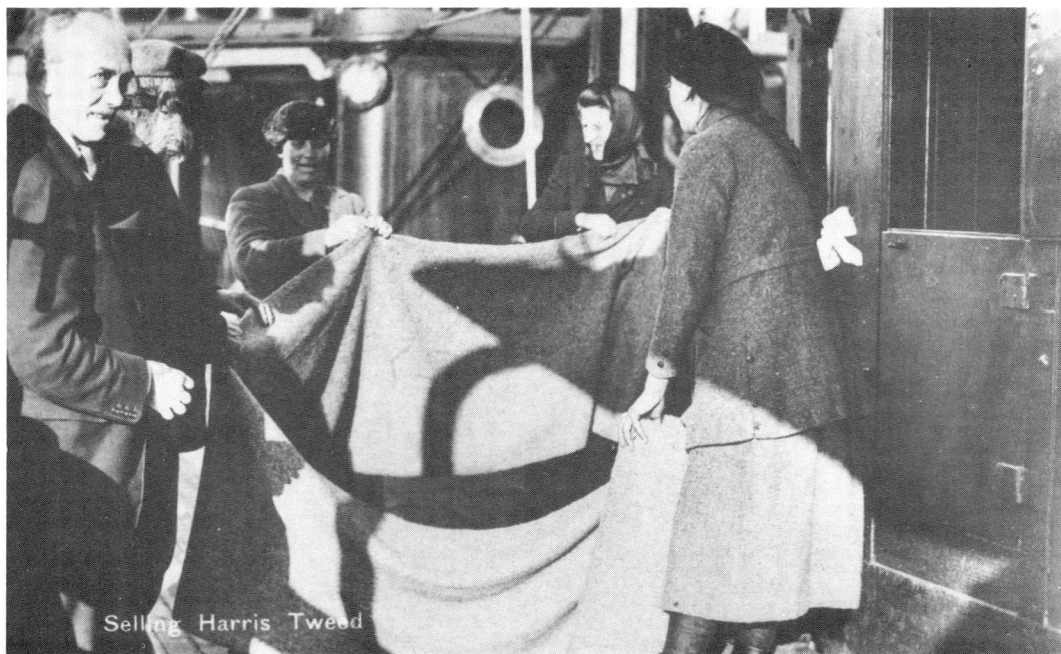

20. 'Selling Harris Tweed.' *"...met a number of boats containing women selling home-made Harris Tweed. It looked very good and several passengers bought some for 3/3d per yard. It takes 7 yards for a suit and 8 yards for a dress."*

We then passed out of the entrance, which in the evening looked grander than when we had arrived two hours previously, and steamed to Lochmaddy arriving about 7 o'clock. We bring up at the pier which, like Dunvegan, is capacious, and we landed to see the sights which consisted of an Hotel - the 'Loch Maddy' - and an odd house or two. Everything looked very desolate.

Mr. Peter Morrison, the Government Official whose duty it is to settle disputes among the crofters, went ashore here having found us at Dunvegan. He seems to be very popular among the Highlanders, or crofters, and the inhabitants of this part of the world.

We found that there was an element of risk going through the Harris Straits in the dark, so we anchored in Lochmaddy for the night, intending to start at 2.00 a.m. The evening was again enjoyable - singing and blind man's-bluff were in full swing - but at the first effort the latter game came to an early finish as they completely lost five of the hiding side!

Tonight my bed quarters have been fixed in a more comfortable position, viz: - on top of the bath in the smoke room. There are two others in the room, a doctor and the parson of St. Kilda being my stable companions".

21. 'Loch Maddy, North Uist.' "...steamed to Lochmaddy arriving at about 7 o'clock. We bring up at the pier which, like Dunvegan, is capacious, and we landed to see the sights which consisted of an Hotel - the 'Loch Maddy' - and an odd house or two. Everything looked very desolate.

"I would like to draw a veil over the passage from Harris to St. Kilda. It was night. The Atlantic was rather unruly, and many of the passengers were very uncomfortable." [The Revd. Roderick Lawson: from his one penny, 24 page pamphlet "Flight to St. Kilda" written after his voyage to the island aboard the S.S. *Hebrides* in July, 1902]

4. To St. Kilda!

Thursday 28th August

"ROSE EARLY in the morning at about 4 o'clock and made our way out of Lochmaddy coasting, or rather passing, close to the numerous tree-less desolate isles along the coast to the Sound of Harris. Here we stayed some time before the Captain thought fit to pass through the Sound which was through a channel amid numerous large and small islands which exist all along here. The actual channel which we pass through into the broad Atlantic on the way to St. Kilda is very narrow and the weather was very dirty and we had every promise of a fairly rough trip in misty weather.

Breakfast was served just after we got through the Sound but very few had any - I had none. The seas were such as I had never seen before and I spent most of the time in the stern hanging over the side, otherwise watching the recording log, in fact I was practically touching the indicator all the way. I did not much care at one time if I was in the briny or on the ship - I felt bad, very, very bad; apparently I was not alone in this feeling.

A first-class dinner (not me!) was served just as we arrived at St. Kilda. We approached St. Kilda, after a journey of 57 miles from the Sound of Harris, in a mist, and suddenly we saw the Isle loom out of it.

It was perfectly grand; high bluff cliff surmounted with a thick mist. The bay we entered was protected by high, grand granite bluffs and one isle looked like a big mound rising out of the sea covered with gannets. As we approached our anchorage we could see the inhabited part of the island and gradually, as we drew up, we saw 4 or 5 boats come out from the stone pier erected by the Government.

We also saw sheep of a small species feeding on the hills. The hills also seemed to be covered with mounds which looked like stone haycocks and there were a large number of mounds of peat in addition.

Borreray and Stacks, St. Kilda.

22. 'Boreray and stacks, St. Kilda.'. A sepia printed postcard with the purple cachet on reverse: 'St. Kilda 21 Aug 1934'.

23. 'Borrera, Gannet Stack. *A black and white printed postcard produced circa 1904 from a Victorian photograph taken by D. Whyte of Inverness.*

Landing Stores at St. Kilda.

24. 'Landing Stores at St. Kilda.' *An anonymously produced sepia-printed postcard circa 1910. "... we saw 4 or 5 boats come out from the stone pier erected by the Government."*

25. 'The Fairy Cave, St. Kilda.' *An anonymously produced black and white printed postcard circa 1908. "The hills also seemed to be covered with mounds which looked like stone haycocks..."*

The village is in a semi-circular formation facing the bay - fronting a so-called street of about 12 to 15 feet, made of slabs of granite with a granite stone wall in front dividing the street from the cultivated portion of the island, which consists of about 20 acres. The crops - principally of potatoes and barley - were not ripe to our idea of ripeness but the St. Kilda people said they were now going to start their harvest. I should say that the crops will not be very remunerative, but the people seem satisfied.

26. 'Village and Bay, St. Kilda.' *A fine sepia photographic postcard showing the majestic curve of Village Bay. No publisher's credit, but the words 'British Made' and the style of printing suggests a publication date just after the Great War when foreign goods were still shunned. The actual photograph was taken before the building of the pier in 1901.*

27. 'St. Kilda. The Bay from the South.' *A real photographic black and white postcard produced by J.B. White of Dundee in the 1960s from a photograph taken in the 1880s.*

The houses were, as a rule, built of stone and many were roughly put together. One or two, at the end of the line of cottages which numbered 16 in all, were fairly well built.

In one of these a 3 day old baby lived, but the mother did not do as the books say - wait for 4 days before clothing it to see if it got over the period of Tetanus which all new-born babies of St. Kilda suffer from. She was exceedingly proud of it and treated it in the same way as the proudest mainland mother would. It was her first. Dr. Cameron of Glasgow University came with us on purpose to inspect this baby and examine it in view of the reported epidemic amongst these young children. He tried two years ago to be present at the birth of one but he could not land. He carefully examined this 3 day old child and came to the conclusion that it showed no signs whatsoever of any disease and, I fancied, that the whole idea was fancy.[4]

In several of the houses which I saw the spirit of cleanliness did not seem to predominate - their ashes and offal seemed to be thrown out of the door, or just over the wall opposite.

There was one stone hut, occupied by an old woman about 80 years of age, which was specially built of loose stones and covered with earth, and on entering the hut I nearly fell into the peat store which was a basin shaped pan dug out of the floor; this place was divided off from her sitting room by a rough partition. Her room was the climax - almost dark. She asked for a match to light her lamp. The light was not much better when the lamp was lit and the smell was awful - dirt, filth and peat smoke all combined. Thank God, the peat was slightly overpowering.

The old woman knew very little English, only *No farder, no mudder, no brudder, no sister.'* She was, as I saw, an octogenarian.[5] After giving her some coppers we again reached the fresh air and passed on, buying some birds eggs which seemed plentiful so far as gannets, fulmars and puffins were concerned.

[4]Official records show that on 24 August 1913 a girl, Kirsty, was born to Donald and Ann (nee MacQueen) Gillies of Cottage number 14, St. Kilda. She contracted mumps at the age of 11 and died on 10 January 1925.

[5]Undoubtedly the writer was meeting Rachel MacCrimmon who lived in the thatched cottage alongside Cottage number 1. She died the following year (1914) aged 81 years. Many more personal details of most of the people living in St. Kilda at this time can be found in David Quine's second book, **'St. Kilda Portraits'** (1988).

28. 'Main Street, St. Kilda' A black and white printed
postcard with the unidentified mark 'D.R.M.', issued circa
1909.

29. *The Village street - a private, sepia photograph taken circa 1900.*

The Manse and School are situated together near the landing-place, and here we said good-bye to the Reverend MacArthur, who we brought with us after he had enjoyed a well deserved holiday at his home in Tiree, and the *Daily Mirror* wireless man, Mr. Figuardo, a Portuguese full of life and vigour, and for a young man of about 20, I pity him for the next four months, which is the period he is stopping here.

30. 'Church, School & Manse. St. Kilda.' *A pre-1910 printed postcard marked 'D.R.M'. These early buildings are still standing, but the Manse now serves the needs of the military whilst the church - beautifully restored - remains permanently open for those wishing to use it for its intended purpose. On the first Sunday in August 1992, passengers and crew of the 'J.D.L.' attended a moving service conducted by David Quine, former School Chaplain at Monkton Combe Junior School near Bath and author of two fascinating and informative books about St. Kilda.*

The wireless station which is placed near the Post office, consists of two poles with the usual apparatus connected to the Post Office which is the next house to the Manse. This Post Office is kept by one Neil Ferguson, a canny Kildonian, and consists of two rooms; and such rooms! One was used as a store for flour, and I should think had not been cleaned for years, and the other was the Post Office. At the corner was the wireless apparatus, and by the window was a table on which the Post Office materials were kept; a pad and a stamp for the St. Kilda postmark. I stamped a lot of postcards and some blank ones with it.

The Post Master had a smoke with me and he told me that they had not any difficulty in posting letters, only the letters take their time in getting to the mainland, some by trawlers in the winter and some by a bag being thrown into the sea, afterwards to be picked up. Very few, he said, go astray.

The inhabitants seem generally delighted to see us and welcomed us everywhere. I was particularly struck by the beauty of some of the female Kildonians; they were nearly all dark, with no (or few of them had) high cheek-bones, and with a set of red handkerchiefs round their necks and dark shawls round their heads. They had gloves for sale and also homespun cloth. We saw some women weaving homespun; they pluck the wool from the sheep and work it.

32. 'Village, St. Kilda.' *A real sepia photographic postcard in the 'McCallum, Orme & Co. Ltd.'s Series' issued in 1930, just in time for Freda Carter to send it to her sister in Pilling, near Preston, Lancashire, with the message 'Last Greetings from St. Kilda'. It was one of the many pieces of mail to be stamped with the St. Kilda cancellation on the final day. The small, white building, to the left of the picture, functioned as the 'St. Kilda Post Office' from 1913 to 1930 under the official postmaster Neil Ferguson. Today, visitors and 'residents' may apply one or all of three private cachets to their envelopes and postcards, but the official St. Kilda postmark no longer exists, and any departing helicopter or vessel will carry the mail to the next port of call where the postage stamp will receive its official Royal Mail cancellation.*

33-34. *Two photographs taken outside the Factor's House in the early 1900s. One of these pictures appeared in a 1988 book about St. Kilda where all four persons were identified, the little boy in the centre being named as 'Calum MacDonald' (1908-1979). Assuming that the boy was about three years old at the time, this dates the photograph to around 1911. The second picture recently turned up on a single page from an old photograph album, pasted down along with four other pictures taken in St. Kilda. Each picture has a handwritten caption and the date '1902' heads the page and is repeated twice, leaving us with the small problem of identity if the year '1902' is correct!*

35. *A private photograph of a group of St. Kildan women and children, and one male islander, taken in July 1901.*

The men were mostly dark like the women. There were some red-haired - these were mostly over 40 and looked like a distinct breed, probably of Norwegian or Norse origin. They were not particularly good-looking like their dark brothers.

36. 'St. Kilda's Parliament.' *An anonymously produced black and white printed postcard circa 1908.*

37. 'Some Natives, St. Kilda.' *A black and white printed postcard issued anonymously circa 1902.*

The children looked very healthy, but I am sorry to say that there is in them a habit of trying to get a sort of backsheesh out of everyone and never leaving you alone. The girls were well dressed and seemed to be satisfied with sweets and what I particularly observed - to their credit - was that when you offered them out of a box they only took *one,* and the older women did the same. This seemed a change altogether from what we meet with in England and is greatly to the credit of the young Kildonians.

There are several dogs on the island which seem to live together and run about in, as it were, a pack. They heralded our approach to the pier by barking as loudly as they could and seemed, like their masters and mistresses, very pleased to see us. I made friends with one or two, but they were not having much talk to us strangers. They were of a kind of sheep dog breed, a kind of mongrel, Greenland sledge dogs with a bit of Newfoundland dog in them, and one Scotch terrier. I saw no cats in the Isle whilst I was there but I hear there are some.

38. 'Children of St. Kilda' *An anonymously produced black and white printed postcard circa 1908.*

We were disappointed at not seeing the numbers of birds we had read about, but they are for the most part on the other side of the Isle. The common ones seem to be Gannets, Solan Geese, Fulmars, Forked tail Petrel, Big and Lesser black backed Herring Gull and several other kinds of gulls, but the ones I have named are the common ones. The razor-bill bird is also common.

The fulmar is the most prominent here; they say there are about 10 to 15 thousand pairs nesting here every year. It is a curious bird; from the two openings of the beak it exudes a kind of oil which people collect and sell. They say the birds use it as a means of defence, viz:- when it is attacked it shoots this oil out against its oppressor and it has the desired effect, and I personally should say it would, if my experience of fulmar oil is correct.

The inhabitants catch them by various means and kill them in large quantities for the oil. Their method of catching them, with a horse-hair noose attached to a long rod, is very interesting. They generally put out a sentinel bird and the men watch for him and noose him - they then make easy work with numbers after that. I may say, in passing, that the whole of the island is impregnated with a certain kind of peculiar smell which is put down to the sea-birds. In warm weather, and if the wind is right, you can smell the Isle some miles out at sea.

39. 'Bird Fowling, St. Kilda.' *A real sepia photographic postcard in the 'McCallum, Orme & Co., Ltd's Series' issued in 1929.*

40. 'Returning from the Fulmar Hunt, St. Kilda.' *A photograph taken in the 1880s which re-emerged as a printed postcard in the early years of this century under the trade-mark 'G.W.W.', George Washington Wilson. This example was posted from St. Kilda, in July 1905, to a single lady in Fairfield, Manchester, and carries the cryptic message "I am still considering your offer."*

41. 'Deciphering a Message from the Sea!' *Certainly a strange caption to this black and white printed card with the G.W.W.' trade-mark. Whilst the islanders used their famous 'mail-boat' method to send messages outward, I know of no instance of the method being used to send a reply back to Hirta!*

42. *A multi-view, real photographic postcard circa 1910-1912, produced specifically for the tourist trade. It is marked on the reverse 'Printed abroad' and identified only as 'Series No.3'.*

43. 'Returning from Church, St. Kilda' is the caption on the back of this private photograph taken in July 1901. Assuming it was a Sunday, it would have been inappropriate for the visitors to roam around the island or remain ashore to eat their packed lunches.

There is a lovely little patch of sandy beach on the right of the pier, and our Kildonian boatman said that the floor of the bay was covered with sand. It is very curious if that is so, for I heard nothing of soles &c., being caught there, although other kinds of fish seem to be very numerous.

We left St. Kilda and the whole of the islanders, practically, came down to see us off, the Reverend MacArthur and my friend Figuardo among them. The latter, I think was beginning to look rather glum at the prospect of his remaining practically in durance vile for the next 4 months on the Isle. The girls of the isle gave us a cheer as the steamer left with the good wishes and best of luck from everyone, hoping we should soon return to visit them.

I do not think I want to stay any time at St. Kilda, but I must say that the visit was most interesting and delightful."

44-45. *Two postcards, circa 1960, with the imprint 'Royal Artillery Guided Weapons Range (Hebrides), Benbecula, Western Isles', and produced after their re-occupation of Hirta in 1957. Aircraft 'drops' have been replaced by helicopters!*

46. 'The Lonely Island of St. Kilda. The Landing Stage.' *A printed card, of poor quality, published by 'Charles Beswick, Up-to-date Stationer, Macclesfield', postally used in 1907.*

"When people ask me, *"Is St. Kilda worth seeing?"* I can only answer with Thomas Carlyle. "It is worth seeing but it is not worth *going to see."* It is a bare rocky island, or rather a group of islands, fifty miles beyond the Outer Hebrides, with a row of one-storey cottages a little bit off the beach." [The Revd. Roderick Lawson: from his one penny, 24 page pamphlet "Flight to St. Kilda" written after his voyage to the island aboard the S.S. *Hebrides* in July, 1902]

5. The Return Trip

"HAD A SPLENDID passage to the Sound of Harris, the wind being with us so we did not feel the roll of the Atlantic so much. On passing the Sound several passengers thought they saw an aeroplane. Of course it was a mistake, but it is curious how at least 20 to 30 of the passengers thought they saw one.

We went straight across the Minch to Dunvegan and we drew up in the dark alongside another boat, called the *Plover,* at the pier. It was dark and raining.

As we were to stay some time I went ashore to stretch my legs and found we had to take on board over 800 sheep and lambs from Skye. They had been collected from various crofters in Skye and were being taken to Glasgow and then on to Stirling. There were with them 4 perfect sheep dogs, but we only took one on board with the shepherd, who was a fine tall Highlander from the Perth district, and could talk English as well as the Gaelic. Several of us helped bring the sheep on board and they were stowed away on the 2nd and 3rd decks, leaving room for more to come later on from other ports. The sheep are carried to Glasgow for 6d a head.

Dunvegan Castle looked very proud in the dim light with all the windows lighted up, perhaps, I should say, more grand and weird than in the daytime. We stayed at Dunvegan for the night and left before daybreak, across the Minch again to North Uist.

After we had landed some goods we went on to Carnan in Benbecula. The whole coast or country is nothing but islands and lochs. We shipped some more sheep here - considerable difficult was had in getting the sheep from the rocks on to the ferry boat; it was interesting watching the dog at work and marvellous to see how sure-footed the sheep were on the slippery rocks.

Ferryboats at Carnan Benbecula

47. 'Ferryboats at Carnan, Benbecula.' "...we went on to Carnan in Benbecula. The whole coast or country is nothing but islands and lochs. We shipped some more sheep here..."

We then went South to a lovely little place called Skipport. Here we stayed some one and a half hours unshipping and shipping goods. I had a walk over the heather and collected a few plants, and Biddy took a further and longer one with the most energetic part of the party.

48. 'Loch Skipport, South Uist.' *"We then went South to a lovely little place called Skipport. Here we stayed some one and a half hours unshipping and shipping goods."*

49. 'Cottages at Loch Skipport.' *"We saw two or three crofters' houses, or rather huts. The people all talk Gaelic and apparently no English."*

A school of porpoises were playing in the loch, and from the top of the hill on which I stood in the sunlight the loch looked perfect, with a large number of gulls flying about and quite a number of porpoises. There is a good road to the pier from the country and there is a special breed of goat here also, a kind they say like the mountain goat. We saw two or three crofters' houses, or rather huts. The people all talk Gaelic and apparently no English. We left this beautiful spot by its narrow entrance in the evening.

Lochboisdale, South Uist. There is a rather capacious pier here with two hotels, several houses and a church. This loch again resembles the others we have seen in North and South Uist, and while we were waiting, two or three of the passengers started fishing for the small fish which seem to abound here, called cuddies, but as usual they were too fly to take the hook, although they ate the bait as quickly as it was put on.

The sun was now shining strongly and we could see Mr. Hecla (2,000 feet high) showing well and grand with a wreath of mist a short distance from the top. We left there about 2 o'clock just as we were going to dine. We had, as fish, a salmon trout; about a pound in weight each fish I should think. They were caught at Carbost Loch and put on board the day previous.

Loch Boisdale, South Uist

50. 'Lochboisdale, South Uist.' "There is a rather capacious pier here with two hotels, several houses and a church. This loch again resembles the others we have seen in North and South Uist, and while we were waiting, two or three of the passengers started fishing for the small fish which seem to abound here..."

After about an hour steaming we ran into Castlebay on Barra - a very pretty place and with a large herring-fishing trade.

It was market day when we arrived and we saw several horses and cattle of all sorts. the horses were, for the most part, small but the people said that they were very strong and stood a lot of work. Lord Lovat's Scouts are all mounted on these animals.

The old castle of the McNeils, named Kisimul Castle, stands at the top of the Bay in ruins, and is a fine and grand ruin which figures in Elizabeth Helme's **'St. Clair of the isles'.** On the other side the Atlantic beats on Barra isle with full force, onto a beach of pure white sand. About a mile from Castlebay town there is an interesting village or collection of pure crofters' huts which we visited.

51. 'Castlebay, Barra, from N.E.' *"After about an hour steaming we ran into Castlebay on Barra - a very pretty place and with a large herring fishing trade."*

52. 'Village of Kentangaval, Barra.' *"About a mile from Castlebay town there is an interesting village or collection of pure crofters' huts which we visited."*

At about 5 o'clock we left Castlebay and steamed again across the Minch to Coll, where we arrived in the dark.

We passed between Coll and Tiree, and thanks to the careful navigation of our Captain we arrived safely. He is, I fancy, a man of iron nerves and one who says very little but does everything well and carefully. He is repeated in this by the most excellent mate - both seem to be a pair who give you every confidence.

On arriving at Coll we started taking in some more sheep and some pigs. The pigs objected to coming on board, but with the persuasive powers of the steamer winch, and a noose around their bodies, they were got on board safely, after making a few objecting grunts. The sheep were lifted on board one by one. We left Coll about 12 o'clock for Tiree where we took in about 30 passengers, all country people going to Glasgow. We also took four horses of the usual type and more sheep. It was about 2 a.m. before we left for Tobermory via the Sound of Mull. We passed the lighthouse at the entrance to Tobermory Bay at about 7 o'clock and found a battleship anchored there - I think it was *H.M.S. Swiftsure*. We did not stay long but left after a few minutes for Oban and arrived at 10 o'clock. There were four battleships and cruisers and two or three gunboats anchored here, H.M.S. *London, Liverpool*, etc. etc.

We stayed about one hour and then left for Colonsay. Here we found more battleships, vis:- *Bulwark, Formidable,* etc. We saw Rear-Admiral Cooper in a launch. We put several golfers ashore, and took in a few, and left after a stay of about 45 minutes for Port Askaig. We arrived about 7 p.m. and the tint of the colour of the trees at this spot was lovely and quite beautiful in the sunset, and so were the white buildings of the place and the Distillery further on.

There is a five to six knot race at this place between Jura and Islay, and we had considerable difficult in getting to the pier against tide and wind. We landed for a few minutes and I picked up a horseshoe on Port Askaig pier, thinking it might bring me a bit of luck which I want badly. We left this place for Glasgow via the Mull of Kintyre. Ugh! The wind doth blow and methinks it will be a bad night - the prospects are bad!

53. 'Port Askaig, Islay.' *"I picked up a horseshoe on Port Askaig pier, thinking it might bring me a bit of luck..."*

We certainly had a dusting round the Mull, but we proved ourselves to be very much improved sailors and survived it. We saw the flashlight on the coast of Ireland - probably the light on Rathlin. After we rounded the Mull we were comparatively on calm water along the coast to Arran and Bute, and so we moved up the Clyde to our destination in Glasgow, where we had started from.

Thus ended the most delightful trip - to St. Kilda and the Outer Hebrides!"

(Whilst this ends the account of the trip to St. Kilda our traveller remained in Scotland for a further three days and continued his diary. Because some of these later observations are brief and readable they are included here.)

6. Some Sight-seeing and then Home

"**O**N LEAVING the *Hebrides* at Broomielaw Quay we took a cab to Queen Street Station and caught the Sunday morning train to Edinburgh where we arrived at 11.30. We went straight to the old Waverley Hotel (Cranston's) in Princes Street and booked our quarters. After having some breakfast we took the train to Leith Docks then the steamer *Lady Morston* to Aberdour on the opposite side of the Forth.

We saw, on our way, some 50 to 60 gun and torpedo boats and some cruisers, and as we left the Docks at Leith a German torpedo boat steamed in and took her quarters at the Quay near the Custom House (give me an English torpedo boat for smartness!). Aberdour seems to be a pretty place with a pretty pier running out making a useful little bay for small boats. The rocks, which slope inwards, seem to be laid out in walks on the right hand facing you coming in.

We landed and had a walk round and met a passenger who was on the *Hebrides* and left us at Oban but we could not avail ourselves of his offered hospitality as the boat started again in half-an-hour's time. Aberdour looks to be suffering from the uncleanliness of a town crowd - papers, banana skins &c., all left on the promenade, makes it look very unattractive to East Anglians, where the authorities of the seaport towns take care to keep the roads and public places clean, especially on a Sunday morning. Aberdour Castle, with its old pigeon-cote in front, is seen on coming to the harbour. The castle is very old with walls 5 to 8 feet thick. Randolph, Earl of Murray (of Bannockburn fame), possessed it.

We got on board the steamer again and went to South Queensferry, passing under the grand Forth Bridge. On our way we passed the Isle of Inchcolm, a small isle of bare rock covered with birds, some Solan Geese &c., and saw the new naval base, Rosyth, on the north side.

On Monday 1st September we decided to go to Leith again and down the Forth to Elie, North Berwick, the Bass Rock, Portobello and the isle of May. Biddy went to see her mother. The sea was a bit choppy and the air splendid. We saw the golf courses at Gullane but did not go near enough to the Bass to see sufficient of the birds there. Every isle seems to have its lighthouse and nothing else on it. Elie is a nice watering-place with an excellent golf-course. I got back to Leith at 7 o'clock, met Biddy and after some dinner went to the Palace Music Hall, returning home very tired."

"We took a trip in a charabanc to see the sights of Edinburgh. This was well worth the money, 1/6d each, and saves a lot of time. We saw round the Castle, Cathedral, Old Houses of Parliament, John Knox's burial place and his house, The Huntley Old Town House, Masonic Lodge House, Holyrood Palace and Queen Mary's Bath House. It was curious to see the means adopted for drying clothes out of the windows of the upper stories of the houses in the narrow streets. Arthur's Seat and Salisbury Craigs looked grand this morning, what a fine, happy hunting-ground this is for Edinburgh people. We passed, during the drive, numerous large education establishments, public buildings and monuments.

In the afternoon we went to a cinema and saw *'Ivanhoe'*, and in the evening we saw a show at the Royal Music Hall."

Wednesday 3rd September

"We left Edinburgh - Waverley - at 7.45 for home, via Dunbar, Berwick, Newcastle, Durham, York (where we changed), Doncaster, Gainsborough, Lincoln, Ely, Norwich and home via Lowestoft. Arrived back at Beccles at about 7.30 p.m. and glad of it"

The End

GLASGOW AND THE HIGHLANDS.

WEEKLY TOURS
TO THE
WESTERN ISLES
OF SCOTLAND.

BY THE FAVOURITE STEAMER

"DUNARA CASTLE"
(453 TONS).

From GLASGOW (Berth 44 North Side), every THURSDAY, 2 p.m.
From GREENOCK (West Quay), - - Do., 7 p.m.

Cabin Fare for the Round, £1 15s. ; including Meals, £3 5s.
(Breakfast, Dinner, and Tea).
BERTHS IN DECK STATEROOMS 5s. EXTRA.

ST. KILDA.
Extended Tours to this Island on Special Dates.
Cabin Fare for the Voyage, £2 14s. ; including Meals, £4 4s.

Berths secured on application to
MARTIN ORME & CO., 20 Robertson Street, GLASGOW.
Telegraphic Address—"ISLESMAN, GLASGOW."

54. The Edwardian cover of Martin Orme's Western Isles brochure.

To St. Kilda aboard *'Dunara Castle'*

"Weekly Tours to the Western Isles of Scotland by the favourite steamer 'Dunara Castle' (453 tons). From Glasgow (Berth 44 North Side) every Thursday at 2 p.m. St. Kilda: Extended Tours to this island on Special Dates. Cabin Fare for the voyage, £2.14s.; including meals £4.4s."

Thus Martin Orme & Co. of Robertson Street, Glasgow, advertised their service to the Hebrides and St. Kilda in a 24 page brochure issued at the beginning of this century.

By the early 1920s the price had risen to £10 and the cost of a berth in a Four-Berthed Room was an extra 2/6d or 5/- if in a Deck Cabin.

On 21 August 1930, *Dunara Castle* left Greenock for St. Kilda, making all her usual calls along the route. On Wednesday 27 August at 4.30 p.m. she anchored in Village Bay and when the ship sailed at noon the next day it was all over; St. Kilda had been evacuated.

55. S.S. Dunara Castle. Dunara Castle began her sea-life in 1875 with Martin Orme & Co. of Glasgow, and was perhaps the best known of all the ships that sailed around the West Highlands delivering and collecting cargo. In the summer she took on passengers, and many a Victorian traveller saw the islands of the St. Kilda group from this vessel. Both the Hebrides and the Dunara Castle helped in the evacuation of St. Kilda, and until the outbreak of war they continued to make trips to the island, as the message and cachet on many a 1930s postcard testifies. In 1929 the separate firms of McCallum and Orme combined and Dunara Castle and Hebrides became 'sister' ships. In 1948 McCallum, Orme & Co. Ltd., passed to David MacBrayne Ltd., and Dunara Castle sailed her last voyage around the Highlands. She was scrapped later the same year.

56-57. *Passengers aboard Dunara Castle prior to departure for St. Kilda, July 1901.*

58-59. *At Bunessan, Mull, July 1901. Bunessan was a regular port of call for the Dunara Castle and the photographer appears to have persuaded most of his fellow St. Kilda-bound passengers to stretch their legs and pose for this picture.*

60. *A view of the pier at Tarbert, Harris, in 1901. "The steamer's route from Tiree northwards alternates. One week it is via the West of Skye to Harris, and returning via the Outer Isles; the other week it is via the Outer Isles, and returning via West of Skye ... On Saturday afternoon the Steamer moors at Tarbert Pier. There is a thriving village, with two churches and an excellent hotel, and a number of shops where real Harris tweed can be bought." (Dunara Castle brochure).*

61. *Obbe, Harris, 1901. "Leaving Tarbert at 3 a.m. on Monday, the course is along the bleak coast of South Harris ... The Steamer anchors at Obbe, in the Sound of Harris. When the Steamer goes to St. Kilda she proceeds from Obbe westward to the lonely islands, 50 miles away." (Dunara Castle brochure).*

62-66. *A selection of photographs taken from the deck of the Dunara Castle as she approached Village Bay, summer, 1901. "The Steamer goes occasionally to this remote group of islands. Then she proceeds from Obbe westward through the devious channel to the Atlantic. The aspect of the St. Kildan group of islands, with their abrupt peaks and the stupendous cliffs, is imposingly sublime." (Dunara Castle brochure).*

67-70. Snapshots of St. Kilda taken during the summer of 1901.

"St. Kilda, like Iona, has become the happy hunting-ground of the Lowland tourist, and nearly every year some irresponsible book or magazine article, founded on a week's observation plus a *Kodak* camera, is added to the "literature" of the subject. When we were last in Eriskay where, during the two years of our previous absence only three strangers had landed, we observed from the newspapers that during the fortnight of our solitary stay in that lonely island, over 300 visitors had arrived in St. Kilda. The natives are deteriorating under the foolish treatment of those who "take an interest" in them; who bring them presents of silver teaspoons, confectionery, silk aprons, mantelpiece ornaments, and silk handkerchiefs of tartans belonging to no clan in the island." [Prophetic words from Ada Goodrich Freer in **'Outer Isles'** 1902]

ABOUT THE AUTHOR

Bob Charnley was born in Lancashire in 1940 and educated at Stonyhurst College and St. Augustine's College, Co. Cavan. He joined the Metropolitan Police in the early 1960s, serving in central London and at the Palace of Westminster. In 1968 he returned to his native county and continued his career as a detective with Lancashire Constabulary. His passion for the Highlands and Islands of Scotland extends to the field of 'collecting', and Bob has many thousands of early photographic images of the region, including a unique record of a Victorian 'Scottish Grand tour' taken by a Tunbridge Wells doctor. The success of a major three month exhibition of these particular 1889 photographs, held at the national Library of Scotland in Edinburgh in 1989, resulted in the publication of the highly acclaimed **'The Summer of '89'.**

By the same author:

Barra and Vatersay
- a Traveller's Guide   Hebridean Enterprises 1981
                                                        (now out of print)
Last Greetings from St. Kilda   Stenlake & McCourt 1989
                                                        (reprinted twice, 1992)
The Summer of '89   Maclean Press 1991
Shipwrecked on Vatersay!   Maclean Press 1992
The Western Isles: A Postcard Tour
1. Barra to North Uist   Maclean Press 1992

Joint author:
                        Bob Charnley and Roger Miket:
Skye: A Postcard Tour   Maclean Press 1992